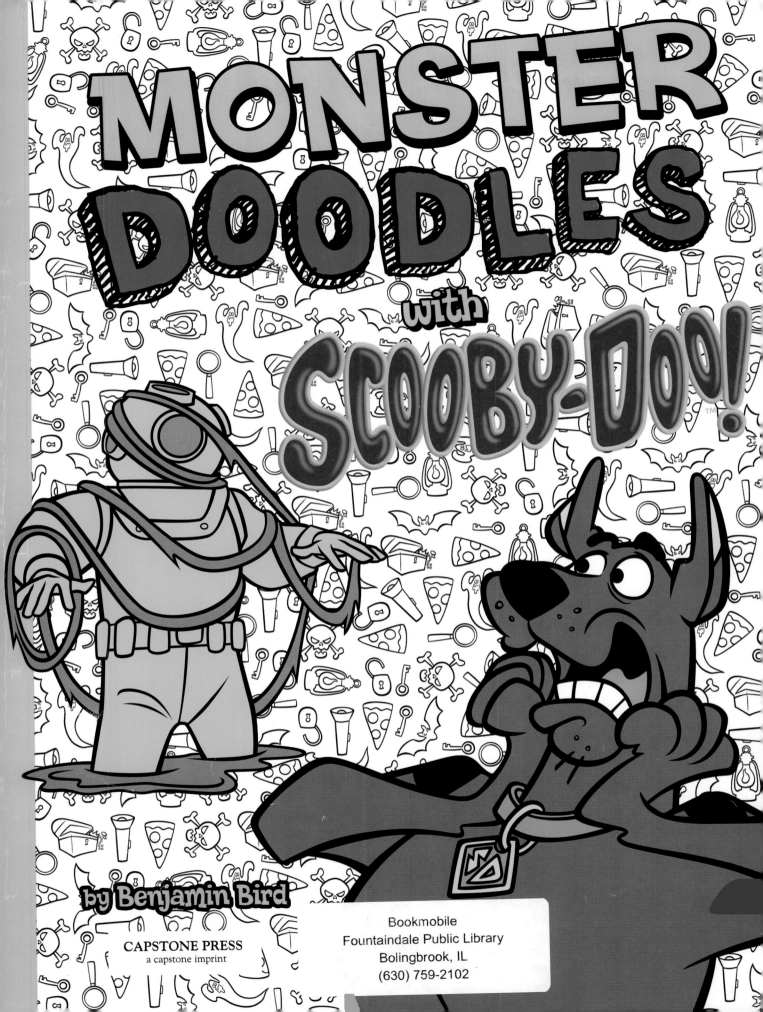

MONSTER DOODLES

with SCOOBY-DOO! ™

by Benjamin Bird

CAPSTONE PRESS
a capstone imprint

Scooby-Doodles
are published in 2017 by Stone Arch Books,
A Capstone Imprint
1710 Roe Crest Drive,
North Mankato, Minnesota 56003
www.mycapstone.com

CAPS38614

Cataloging-in-Publication Data is available on the Library of Congress website.

ISBN: 978-1-5157-3406-2 (hardcover)
ISBN: 978-1-5157-3411-6 (eBook)

Summary: Draw and create MONSTER doodles with Scooby-Doo!

Designed by Lori Bye

Capstone Studio: Karon Dubke, (supplies) 5; Scott Neely: (sketches) 8-9, 10-11,
14-15, 16-17, 18-19, 20-21, 22-23, 25, 27, 28-29

All other illustrations not listed above are credits to Warner Brothers

Printed and bound in the USA
010052S17CG

TABLE OF CONTENTS

LIKE, HELP, SCOOBS!

Zoinks! Think art is truly terrifying? Well, think again.

Like solving a great mystery, drawing just takes a little planning and practice. In *Monster Doodles with Scooby-Doo!*, you'll discover tools, tips, and tricks to make doodling a scary-good experience.

Use this book for daily doodling fun! In your own sketchbook, follow Scooby and the gang through warm-up exercises, pattern practice, and step-by-step drawing instructions.

You'll unmask your inner artist in no time!

TOOLS

Scooby and the gang need proper tools, like flashlights and magnifying glasses, to solve mysteries. With a few basic tools, you can doodle like a pro!

ERASER

Ruh-roh! Don't fear mistakes. An eraser can solve most problems.

RULER

Even the shakiest hand can draw a straight line with a ruler.

PENCILS

Jinkies! Worried about making mistakes? Sketch outlines of your doodles first. They're great for detailed coloring, too!

COLORED MARKERS

Don't get lost in the dark! Brighten up your doodles with multicolored markers.

FINE-TIP MARKERS

Any great detective knows details matter — the same goes for great doodlers! Use fine-tip, waterproof markers to give your drawings scary-good details.

MEET MYSTERY INC.

SCOOBY-DOO

SKILLS: Loyal; super snout
BIO: This happy-go-lucky hound
avoids scary situations at all
costs, but he'll do anything for a
Scooby Snack!

SHAGGY ROGERS

SKILLS: Lucky; healthy appetite
BIO: This laid-back dude would rather look for grub than search for clues, but he usually finds both!

FRED JONES, JR.

SKILLS: Athletic; charming
BIO: The leader and oldest member of the gang. He's a good sport — and good at them, too!

DAPHNE BLAKE

SKILLS: Brains; beauty
BIO: As a sixteen-year-old fashion queen, Daphne solves her mysteries in style.

VELMA DINKLEY

SKILLS: Clever; highly intelligent
BIO: Although she's the youngest member of Mystery Inc., Velma's an old pro at catching crooks.

GANGWAY!

What does starting a doodle and escaping a deadly zombie have in common? Never walk — RUN!! Use these warm-up exercises to get off to a fast start!

In your sketchbook, doodle as many
ZOMBIE TEETH
as you can in five minutes!

In your sketchbook, doodle all of these
EVIL EYES,
and then create some of your own!

DISCOVER PATTERNS

To crack a case, great detectives look for patterns of evidence. Doodling patterns — repeating the same design over and over — can help you discover a path to drawing success.

IN YOUR SKETCHBOOK, USE THESE DOODLES TO CREATE YOUR OWN PATTERN OF MONSTER FOOTPRINTS.

IN YOUR SKETCHBOOK, CREATE A PATTERN OF BLOODTHIRSTY VAMPIRE BATS!

Why won't anyone kiss Dracula?

BAT BREATH!

FIND CLUES

Scooby and the gang focus on finding small clues to solve big mysteries. Grid drawing is a great way to break a large illustration into smaller, more manageable parts.

TOOLS:
Ruler
Pencil
Paper
Fine-tip marker
Eraser

1. Using the ruler and pencil, draw a grid of squares like the one on page 13 (seven columns and seven rows).

2. Next, choose a square of the pirate to draw with the fine-tip marker.

3. Once you've finished drawing one square, start on another. And then another and another!

4. When you've finished drawing all the squares, use the eraser to remove the grid from your pirate drawing!

REDBEARD'S GHOST!

What's a pirate's favorite subject in school?

ARRRRRRRT!

FOLLOW LEADS

The Mystery Inc. gang follows a series of leads, or clues, to solve every case. In the pages to come, follow each series of instructions to create groovy drawings.

SHAGGY!

1. With a pencil, lightly outline the main shapes of Shaggy's body and head.

2. Using the outline as your guide, draw Shaggy's outfit, including his shirt, pants, and shoes. Add his ears and fingers, too!

3. Then, give Shaggy some details! Add his eyes, eyebrows, mouth, floppy hair, and scruffy beard. Afterward, erase any unnecessary lines and fix any last-minute mistakes.

4. ADD COLOR!
Outline your drawing with a fine-tip, black marker. Then use colored markers to bring Shaggy to life!

5. GRAB A SNACK!!
(Repeat step 5 until finished . . . or full!)

SCOOBY!

This mystery-solving hound has a nose for tracking down monsters — when he's not running the other way! Doodle Scooby-Doo in four easy steps.

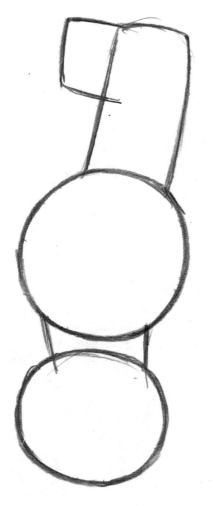

1. With a pencil, lightly outline the main shapes of Scooby's body and head.

2. Using the outline as your guide, draw Scooby's front and back legs. Add his ears, too!

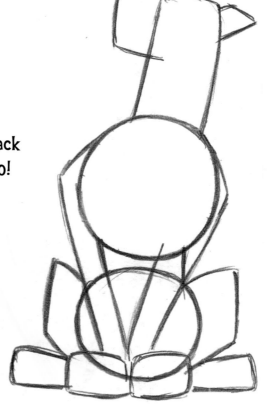

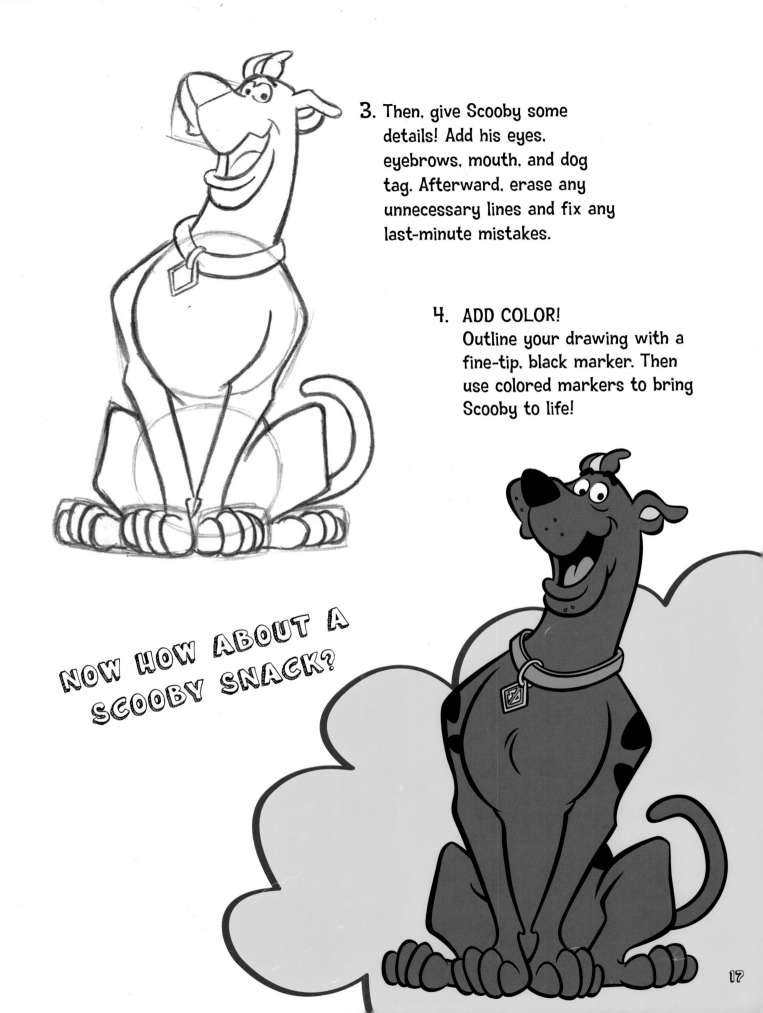

3. Then, give Scooby some details! Add his eyes, eyebrows, mouth, and dog tag. Afterward, erase any unnecessary lines and fix any last-minute mistakes.

4. ADD COLOR! Outline your drawing with a fine-tip, black marker. Then use colored markers to bring Scooby to life!

NOW HOW ABOUT A SCOOBY SNACK?

GHOST CLOWN!

Ghost Clown had Mystery Inc. scared silly — until they discovered this crazy clown was just a clever crook in disguise!

Drawing faces can be frightening, too. Follow these steps to turn doodling fears into doodling fun!

1. Begin any face by identifying the basic shapes, including half circles, ovals, and triangles. Remember: sketch lightly with a pencil at first! You can always erase any unnecessary lines or mistakes later on.

2. Next, use the basic shapes as an outline for the remainder of your drawing. For the Ghost Clown, add eyes above the nose and tufts of hair to the sides of the head.

3. Then, add the Ghost Clown's mouth. At this point, begin to customize your drawing. Want a happy clown? An evil clown? Or maybe a sad clown? The choice is up to you!

4. Fill in the mouth, add pupils and any other facial features. Once you're finished, erase any unnecessary lines or pencil marks.

5. Finally, outline your Ghost Clown with a fine-tip marker and color!

CREEPERS!

Why was the clown mad?

BECAUSE HE BROKE HIS FUNNY BONE!

SNOW GHOST!

When a local innkeeper dressed up as an evil Yeti, he left resort goers shaking in their ski boots!

Don't let drawing this Snow Ghost give you cold feet. Follow these easy steps.

1. Lightly sketch the main shapes of the Snow Ghost with a pencil. Notice how the monster's head is shaped exactly like an egg!

2. Then, add details to your outline, such as fur, fingers, and abominable toes.

3. Next, add facial features. The Snow Ghost's gruesome grin could send a chill down anyone's spine!

4. ADD COLOR!
Outline your drawing with a fine-tip, black marker. Then fill in the fur with any color you prefer!

THEN...
Doodle an icy landscape for your Snow Ghost to haunt!

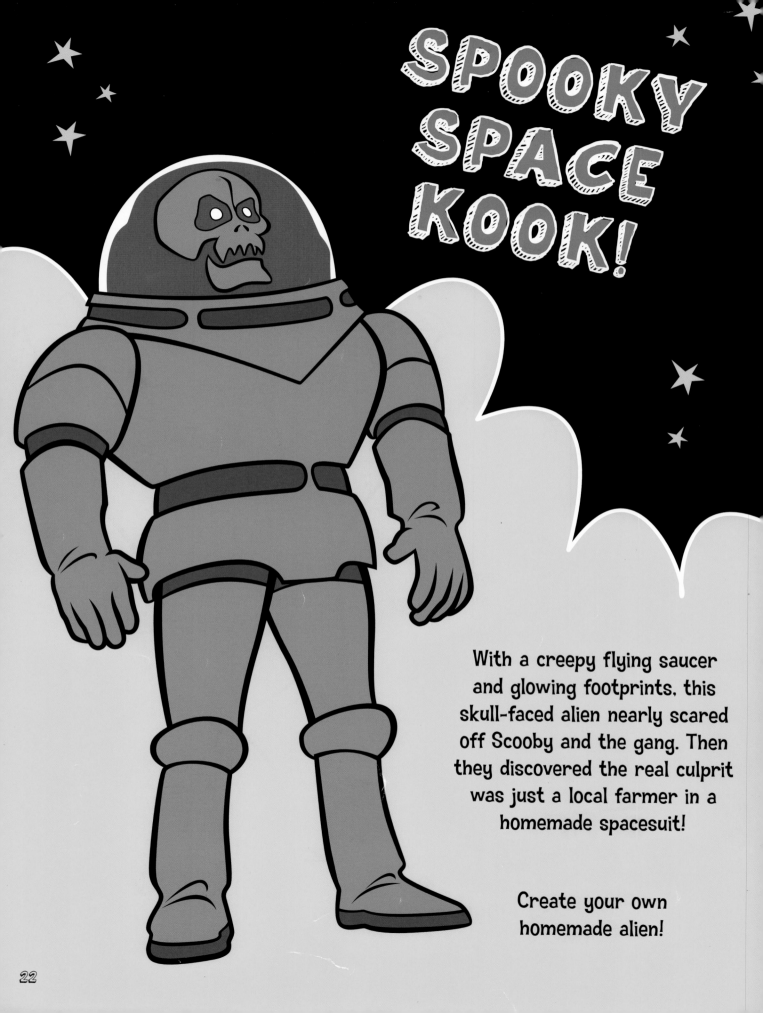

SPOOKY SPACE KOOK!

With a creepy flying saucer and glowing footprints, this skull-faced alien nearly scared off Scooby and the gang. Then they discovered the real culprit was just a local farmer in a homemade spacesuit!

Create your own homemade alien!

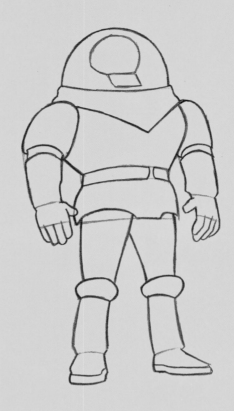

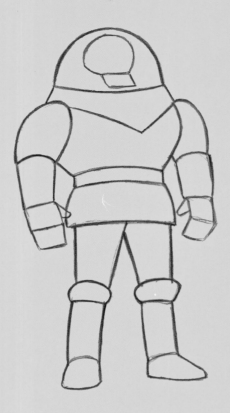

1. First, lightly sketch your Spooky Space Kook with a pencil. Remember, you will have to erase some lines later on!

2. Next, add details to your creepy creature, such as fingers, a belt, and boots.

3. Finally, give your monster a skull face. Or, get creative and draw a spooky face of your own! Erase any extra lines and add color, if desired.

THEN . . .

Doodle an out-of-this-world landscape for your outer-space monster!

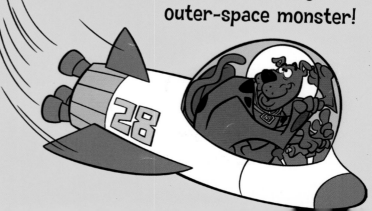

The MUMMY!

ZOINKS! Think your drawing skills are cursed? Think again!

Follow the steps to take down this ancient mummy in no time!

1. With a pencil, sketch the outline of the mummy's body. Note: this outline can be used to create other monsters as well, like Frankenstein's monster!

2. Begin adding bandages to the mummy's shape. Vary the width of the bandages — make some thick and some thin.

3. Fill in the eyes and mouth and complete the remaining bandages. Then erase any extra lines and finish with colored markers.

THAT'S A WRAP!

GHOST DIVER!

A boat-stealing seaman, Captain Cutler, scared off townspeople with his ghostly get-up, but he couldn't fool Mystery Inc. Those meddling kids quickly discovered his deep-sea scam.

Learn to draw this deceptive diver!

1. Begin by outlining the basic shapes of the Ghost Diver's uniform.

2. Next, add details to the diver's helmet and suit.

3. Cover your diver in gruesome strands of seaweed and color!

G-G-G-G-GHOST!

27

THE GYPSY'S
CRYSTAL BALL

Mystery Inc. discovered this fortune-teller was nothing but a fake. But one thing's for sure: follow these steps, and you'll create your own crystal ball in no time!

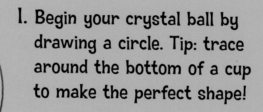

1. Begin your crystal ball by drawing a circle. Tip: trace around the bottom of a cup to make the perfect shape!

2. Create the base for your crystal ball.

3. Next, decorate the base of your crystal ball with fancy jewels. Use a ruler to make straight lines, if desired.

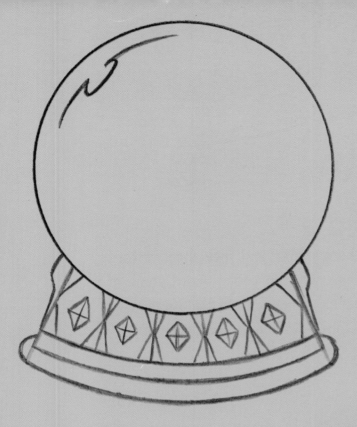

4. Add a few last-minute touches, and then create your own freaky fortune inside!

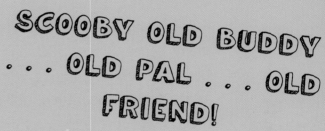

SCOOBY OLD BUDDY ... OLD PAL ... OLD FRIEND!

Benjamin Bird

Benjamin Bird is a children's book editor and freelance writer from St. Paul, Minnesota. He has written books about some of today's most popular characters, including Batman, Superman, Wonder Woman, Scooby-Doo, Tom & Jerry, and many more.

Scott Neely

Scott Neely has been a professional illustrator and designer for many years. Since 1999, he's been an official Scooby-Doo and Cartoon Network artist, working on such licensed properties as Dexter's Laboratory, Johnny Bravo, Courage The Cowardly Dog, Powerpuff Girls, and more. He has also worked on Pokemon, Mickey Mouse Clubhouse, My Friends Tigger & Pooh, Handy Manny, Strawberry Shortcake, Bratz, and many other popular characters. He lives in a suburb of Philadelphia and has a scrappy Yorkshire Terrier, Alfie.

Are you thinking what I'm thinking?

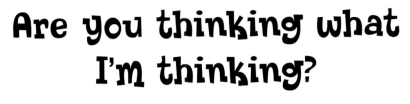
Discover more

SCOOBY-DOODLES!

Only from Capstone!

The fun doesn't stop here!